BE NOT

TROUBLED

BE NOT TROUBLED

RONALD A. RASBAND

DESERET
BOOK

Salt Lake City, Utah

Interior images: page vi, Ben Klea on Unsplash; page 4, Min An/Pexels; page 7, Eberhard Grossgasteiger/Life of Pix; page 8, Markus Spiske/Pexels; page 13, Eberhard Grossgasteiger/Life of Pix; page 21, Esteban Amaro on Unsplash; page 26, Dan Maisey on Unsplash; page 30, Eberhard Grossgasteiger/Life of Pix; page 33, Pixabay/Pexels; page 38, courtyardpix/Shutterstock.com; page 42, martinklass/Pixabay; page 50, Sergey Nivens/Shutterstock.com; page 55, Pixabay/Pexels; page 62, Sandra Cunningham/Shutterstock.com; page 68, Pascal van de Vendel on Unsplash; page 75, bogumil/Shutterstock.com; page 82, kareni/Pixabay; page 87, Ingmar on Unsplash; page 90, rdonar/Shutterstock.com; page 97, Alexey Repka/Shutterstock.com; page 102, David P Baileys/Shutterstock.com; page 106, Rido Alwarno/Pexels.

Visit us at deseretbook.com

Library of Congress Cataloging-in-Publication Data
(CIP data on file)
ISBN 978-1-62972-889-6

Printed in the United States of America
Publishers Printing, Salt Lake City, UT

10 9 8 7 6 5 4 3 2 1

CONTENTS

INTRODUCTION

"THESE ARE MY DAYS"

We live in perilous times. Rage, calamity, and commotion swirl about us. *Rage, calamity,* and *commotion* are sobering words, but our time was clearly prophesied by prophets of old.

In 2 Timothy, the Apostle Paul foretold of our day: "This know also, that in the last days perilous times shall come. For men shall be lovers of their own selves, covetous, boasters, proud, blasphemers, disobedient to parents, unthankful, unholy, . . . lovers of pleasures more than lovers of God" (2 Timothy 3:1–2, 4).

Nephi prophesied of the condition of the hearts of the people in these, the last days: "For behold, at that day shall [the devil] rage in the hearts of the children of men, and stir them up to anger against that which is good. And others [members] will he pacify, and lull them away into carnal security, that they will say: All is well in Zion; yea, Zion prospereth, all is well—and thus the devil cheateth their souls, and leadeth them away carefully down to hell" (2 Nephi 28:20–21).

Being cheated "down to hell" is an ominous conclusion to a life filled with promise since the pre-earth days when we shouted for joy to come to earth and choose life eternal by righteousness. Yet the deceit of the devil and those enslaved to him lures some away.

Challenges, trials, and tribulation are not new to God's children. They make up much of our mortal experience as we seek to become true disciples of Jesus Christ. The key to withstanding the turmoil is to keep focused on Jesus Christ.

"Be not troubled" means to see with a blessed eternal perspective.

Picture the moment in the Kirtland Temple when Joseph described, "The glory of the Lord shone round about" and then bore this powerful witness of Jesus Christ:

"He lives! For we saw him, even on the right hand of God; and we heard the voice bearing record that he is the Only Begotten of the Father—That by him, and through him, and of him, the worlds are and were created, and the inhabitants thereof are begotten sons and daughters unto God" (D&C 76:19, 22–24).

We are those "sons and daughters unto God."

The Lord spoke to the Church in the early days of the

Restoration, as recorded in the first section of the Doctrine and Covenants: "Wherefore, I the Lord, knowing the calamity which should come upon the inhabitants of the earth, called upon my servant Joseph Smith, Jun., and spake unto him from heaven, and gave him commandments" (D&C 1:17).

If we live those divine laws, we lay a firm foundation to deal with troubles and trials of any proportion. We feel the presence of the Lord and the power of His Atonement to help us, lift us, and heal us. His Atonement was wrought in the vilest of circumstances, with the weight of all our pain on Him alone. From His infinite sacrifice came the capacity for Him to feel what we feel—not just when we sin, but when disappointment, broken dreams, unjust treatment, failure, and chaos seem to consume us.

As Alma counseled, "Whosoever shall put their trust in God shall be supported in their trials, and their troubles, and their afflictions, and shall be lifted up at the last day" (Alma 36:3).

No dispensation has been absolved of heartache, frustration, and failure. Nephi, son of Helaman, saw all around him "lovers of pleasures more than lovers of God." He had misgivings—as we are all prone to do—about his time on earth. Looking back at his ancestors and seeing their time as more glowing than it was, he wrote the following: "Oh, that I could have had my days in the days when my father Nephi first came

WORSHIPPING THE LORD,

PRAYING TO OUR FATHER,

LIVING THE COMMANDMENTS,

and honoring our covenants.

OUR DAYS ARE ABOUT BECOMING

DISCIPLES OF CHRIST

with hope and exaltation ever in our sights.

out of the land of Jerusalem, that I could have joyed with him in the promised land; then were his people easy to be entreated, firm to keep the commandments of God, and slow to be led to do iniquity; and they were quick to hearken unto the words of the Lord—Yea, if my days could have been in those days, then would my soul have had joy in the righteousness of my brethren. But behold, I am consigned that these are my days" (Helaman 7:7–9).

Our days are not about living with ease, having our names up in lights, or being the first to the finish line. Our days are about what happened at the Waters of Mormon as the newly baptized were charged to "bear one another's burdens, . . . mourn with those that mourn; . . . comfort those that stand in need of comfort, and to stand as witnesses of God at all times and in all things, and in all places" (Mosiah 18:8–9).

Our days are about looking a little deeper for the good and building on it, generously complimenting the efforts of others, replacing pessimism with optimism, and finding joy in the work that the Lord has given us. Our days are about worshipping the Lord, praying to our Father, living the commandments, and honoring our covenants. Our days are about becoming disciples of Christ with hope and exaltation ever in our sights.

Church history and the scriptures are replete with accounts of those who lived up to their "day." I have always loved the expression of Oliver Cowdery, who wrote of sitting with Joseph Smith as the young prophet translated the Book of Mormon by the power of revelation. "These were days never to be forgotten," he penned (Joseph Smith—History 1:71, note).

Consider ancient prophets Noah, Abraham, Peter, Lehi, and Enoch. By some standards Enoch was old, not particularly gifted, and he stuttered. But the angels wrote of his ministry: "And so great was the faith of Enoch that he led the people of God, and their enemies came to battle against them; and he spake the word of the Lord, and the earth trembled, and the mountains fled, even according to his command; and the rivers of water were turned out of their course; and the roar of the lions was heard out of the wilderness; and all nations feared greatly, so powerful was the word of Enoch, and so great was the power of the language which God had given him" (Moses 7:13).

Our charge is the same given to all those throughout the history of the world who choose the covenant path: "Be patient in long-suffering and afflictions, that ye may show forth good examples . . . , and I will make an instrument of thee in my hands unto the salvation of many souls" (Alma 17:11).

By divine design, we have been called to the Lord's service leading up to His Second Coming. May we rejoice in our day and be not troubled.

BY DIVINE DESIGN,

we have been called to the

Lord's service leading up to

His Second Coming.

MAY WE REJOICE IN OUR DAY

AND

BE NOT

TROUBLED.

1

FIND REFUGE
FROM FEAR

Some years ago, one of our young married daughters and her husband asked Sister Rasband and me a very important, life-influencing question: "Is it still safe and wise to bring children into this seemingly wicked and frightening world we live in?"

Now, that was an important question for a mom and dad to consider with their dear married children. We could hear the fear in their voices and feel the fear in their hearts. Our answer to them was a firm, "Yes, it's more than okay," as we shared fundamental gospel teachings and our own heartfelt impressions and life experiences.

Fear is not new. The disciples of Jesus Christ, out on the Sea of Galilee, feared the "wind, and the waves" in the dark of the night (Mark 4:37). As His disciples today, we too have fears. Our single adults fear making commitments such as getting married. Young marrieds, like our children, can fear bringing children into an increasingly wicked world. Missionaries fear lots of things, especially approaching strangers. Widows fear going forward alone. Teenagers fear not being accepted; grade schoolers fear the first day of school; university students fear getting their test scores. We fear failure, rejection, disappointment, and the unknown. We fear hurricanes, earthquakes, fires, and even pandemics that ravage the land and our lives. We fear not being chosen, and on the flip side, we fear being chosen. We fear not being good enough; we fear that the Lord has no blessings for us. We fear change, and our fears can escalate to terror. Have I included just about everyone?

Since ancient times, fear has limited the perspective of God's children. I have always loved the account of Elisha in 2 Kings. The king of Syria had sent a legion that "came by night, and compassed the city about" (2 Kings 6:14). Their intent was to capture and kill the prophet Elisha. We read: "And when the servant of the man of God was risen early, and gone forth, behold, an host compassed the city both with horses and chariots. And his servant said unto him, Alas, my master! how shall we do?" (v. 15).

That was fear speaking.

"And [Elisha] answered, Fear not: for they that be with us are more than they that be with them" (v. 16).

But he didn't stop there.

"Elisha prayed, and said, Lord, I pray thee, open his eyes, that he may see. And the Lord opened the eyes of the young man; and he saw: and, behold, the mountain was full of horses and chariots of fire round about Elisha" (v. 17).

We may or may not have chariots of fire sent to dispel our fears and conquer our demons, but the lesson is clear. The Lord is with us, mindful of us, and blessing us in ways only He can do. Prayer can call down the strength and the revelation that we need to center our thoughts on Jesus Christ and His atoning sacrifice. The Lord knew that at times we would feel fear. I have been there and so have you, which is why the scriptures are replete with the Lord's counsel: "Be of good cheer, and do not fear" (D&C 68:6); "Look unto me in every thought; doubt not, fear not" (D&C 6:36); and, "Fear not, little flock" (D&C 6:34).

I love the tenderness of "little flock." In this Church we may be few in number by the way the world counts influence, but when we open our spiritual eyes, we see that "they that be with us are more than they that be with them" (2 Kings 6:16). Our loving Shepherd, Jesus Christ, then continues, "Let earth and hell combine against you, for if ye are built upon my rock, they cannot prevail" (D&C 6:34).

How is fear dispelled? How can we "be not troubled"? For the young lad in 2 Kings, a key was to be standing right next to

Elisha, a prophet of God. He was in good company. We have that same promise. When we listen to President Russell M. Nelson, when we hearken to his counsel, we are standing with a prophet of God. President Nelson has taught: "The more we know about the Savior's ministry and mission—the more we understand His doctrine and what He did for us—the more we know that He can provide the power that we need for our lives" ("Drawing the Power of Jesus Christ into Our Lives," *Ensign*, May 2017). Jesus Christ lives. Our love for Him and His gospel dispels fear. Additionally, our desire to "always have his Spirit" with us (D&C 20:77) will push fear aside for a more eternal view of our mortal lives.

Remember, "they that be with us" on both sides of the veil, those who love the Lord with all their heart, might, mind, and strength, "are more than they that be with them." If we actively trust in the Lord and His ways, if we are engaged in His work, we will not fear the trends of the world or be troubled by them. I plead with you to set aside worldly influences and pressures and seek the Spirit and spirituality in your daily life. Love what the Lord loves—which includes His commandments, His holy houses, our sacred covenants with Him, the sacrament each Sabbath day, our communication through prayer—and you will not be troubled.

The scriptures help us see that eternal view also, and they clearly outline ways to find refuge and renewal. In the Doctrine

Jesus Christ LIVES.

OUR LOVE FOR HIM AND
HIS GOSPEL DISPELS FEAR.

and Covenants we read, "Wherefore, stand ye in holy places, and be not moved, until the day of the Lord come; for behold, it cometh quickly, saith the Lord" (D&C 87:8).

Also, in the Doctrine and Covenants we read: "And in that day shall be heard of wars and rumors of wars, and the whole earth shall be in commotion, and men's hearts shall fail them, and they shall say that Christ delayeth his coming until the end of the earth. And the love of men shall wax cold, and iniquity shall abound. . . . But my disciples shall stand in holy places, and shall not be moved; but among the wicked, men shall lift up their voices and curse God and die. . . . And I said unto them: Be not troubled, for, when all these things shall come to pass, ye may know that the promises which have been made unto you shall be fulfilled" (D&C 45:26–27, 32, 35).

Amidst all the conditions of our day, "be not troubled." I would like to share with you how to do this.

I am struck by the emphasis on "stand in holy places." Temples, homes, and chapels are holy places. The presence of the Spirit and our behavior there make them holy places, sanctuaries from the world (see *Handbook 2: Administering the Church* [2010], 1.4.1).

Let's consider one of these holy places: the temple, the importance of temple worship, and the power of the priesthood manifest in the ordinances of the temple. Know this: the temple will be both a defense and a place of refuge from the growing storms.

I am sure many of you have faced tragedies or events that have brought sadness into your lives. It is during these times that we look for that comforting word, a reassuring promise that all will be well.

President Boyd K. Packer gave such a promise. He said: "When members of the Church are troubled or when crucial decisions weigh heavily upon their minds, it is a common thing for them to go to the temple. It is a good place to take our cares. In the temple we can receive spiritual perspective. There, during the time of the temple service, we are 'out of the world.' . . .

"The Lord will bless us as we attend to the sacred ordinance work of the temples. Blessings there will not be limited to our temple service. We will be blessed in all of our affairs" ("The Holy Temple," *Ensign*, Feb. 1995).

We might ask ourselves, "Am I attending often and using our beautiful temples as a refuge from the storms of life, and as a sanctuary of serenity—seeking Heavenly Father's divine plan for me? Am I building my temple experiences now to help me not only in my life today, but also in the future?"

What temples bring to families and individuals seeking to draw closer to the Lord Jesus Christ and our Father in Heaven, seeking peace in a fractured world, seeking comfort in times of trouble, cannot be calculated.

I have often shared a personal story that happened years ago but brought a lasting change for our family. While I served in an Area Presidency, Sister Rasband and I, along with two of our children, lived in England. We knew serving in England would be a sacrifice for our children, particularly our seventeen-year-old son, who was looking forward to his senior year in high school and would miss many athletic competitions. After an assignment to speak in Preston, we enjoyed an especially meaningful, spiritual experience with our children performing baptismal ordinances in the Preston England Temple. While my son and I were still in the font with tears of joy in our eyes, he put his hand on my shoulder and asked, "Dad, why haven't we ever done this before?"

That day, the power of the temple changed our perspectives. As a family, the spirit of the temple sanctified us. We felt peace and joy that no football tournament or basketball game could bring. We stepped away from the world and were spiritually lifted—it was a lasting, precious, and sacred experience for our family.

As our son and his wife are now raising their children— our grandchildren—and helping them, even as young as they are, to build their temple experiences, they are learning how important the temple is. Let me share a story about their daughter Alina, my granddaughter.

One day, the stake Primary children made a visit to the temple in their area. The temple president and his wife greeted the children at the front door of the temple. Alina went over to the temple matron and touched her white dress and her white shoes and then just stood by her. After a few minutes, the president and his wife went back into the temple. At that time, Alina asked her mother, "Where did the angel go?" (Letter from President David T. Halversen, Orlando Florida Temple President, March 22, 2012). I am so grateful to my son and daughter-in-law for teaching their children about the holy temple.

Years ago, at the Logan Utah Temple Cornerstone Ceremony in 1877, President George Q. Cannon said this: "Every foundation stone that is laid for a temple and every temple completed, lessens the power of Satan on the earth, and increases the power of God and Godliness, moves the heavens in mighty power in our behalf, invokes and calls down upon us the blessings of eternal Gods and those who reside in their presence" (*Millennial Star*, Nov. 12, 1877, 743).

Certainly, in a day and time like we live in, the importance of every temple built and dedicated to the Lord cannot be overstated. The First Presidency and Quorum of the Twelve agonized over closing temples around the world because of the

COVID-19 pandemic, as they did stepping back missionary work and withdrawing Sunday worship services in line with government actions. Opening the temples—at first just for sealings of previously endowed members—was a glorious day. Great are the blessings promised by prophets, seers, and revelators for those who attend the temple.

Our dear and beloved prophet, President Russell M. Nelson, has given this very important counsel about attending the temple: "After we receive our own temple ordinances and make sacred covenants with God, each one of us needs the ongoing spiritual strengthening and tutoring that is possible *only* in the house of the Lord" ("Becoming Exemplary Latter-day Saints," *Ensign*, Nov. 2018).

My much-loved boyhood stake president, President James E. Faust, said: "We unavoidably stand in so many unholy places and are subjected to so much that is vulgar, profane, and destructive of the Spirit of the Lord that I encourage our Saints all over the world, wherever possible, to strive to stand more often in holy places. Our most holy places are our sacred temples. Within them is a feeling of sacred comfort" ("Standing in Holy Places," *Ensign*, May 2005).

To what end and what purpose is all of this focus and emphasis on temples? How does it apply to those of you who will soon be starting careers and families? You who are single or married, worrying about jobs and homes and making a living?

You who are middle-aged and juggling the busy demands of a job, a Church calling, and family? And you who miss having family around you, or who, in later years, are caring for a beloved spouse or ailing parent?

Temple worship is an important pattern for each of us as individuals and as families. It is critical at every stage of your life. If you have yet to be sealed in the temple, continue to seek for that blessing. For those who have been sealed, honor that covenant with your heart, might, mind, and strength.

Let me point you to a passage of scripture in the Doctrine and Covenants: "And again, I will give unto you a pattern in all things, that ye may not be deceived; for Satan is abroad in the land, and he goeth forth deceiving the nations" (D&C 52:14).

The First Presidency extended the following invitation and promise to all the members of the Church: "Where time and circumstances permit, members are encouraged to replace some leisure activities with temple service. All of the ordinances which take place in the house of the Lord become expressions of our belief in that fundamental and basic doctrine of the immortality of the human soul. As we redouble our efforts and our faithfulness in going to the temple, the Lord will bless us" (First Presidency letter, March 11, 2003).

As we consider establishing righteous patterns in our lives, it would be well to remember this admonition from the First Presidency.

The statement on the outside facade of every temple reads: "Holiness to the Lord: The House of the Lord." I testify that all of the temples of the Lord are His sanctuaries here upon the earth.

There have been and will be times when we are unable to attend the temple. Holding a current temple recommend helps us always be worthy. I learned this from my father-in-law, Blaine Twitchell, when he was being cared for by hospice on his death bed. Sister Rasband and I went to visit him, and as we entered his room his bishop was just leaving. We greeted him and I thought, "What a nice bishop. He's here doing his ministering to a faithful member of his ward."

I mentioned to Blaine, "Wasn't that nice of the bishop to come visit?"

Blaine responded, "It was far more than that. I asked for the bishop to come because I wanted my temple recommend interview. I want to go—recommended to the Lord."

"Recommended to the Lord" put a whole new perspective on holding a current temple recommend. When we are "recommended to the Lord," we are confirming our worthiness to enter His holy house. We are standing on holy ground, and that brings us peace of mind.

Because of different situations, we may not always be able

TEMPLE
WORTHINESS

IS AN ANCHOR IN OUR LIVES,

A MEASURE OF OUR LOVE,

RESPECT, AND OBEDIENCE TO

the Lord's way.

to attend the temple as a patron, worker, or member. But we can always be "recommended to the Lord." Temple worthiness is an anchor in our lives, a measure of our love, respect, and obedience to the Lord's way.

The blessings of temple service are generational. Standing in holy places may also be considered standing "in line" with our ancestors and doing the work for them that they cannot do for themselves. We know as Latter-day Saints that temple and family history work is pertinent to our salvation—and the salvation of those who have gone before us. We refer to the feelings that we can have in seeking out our departed ancestors as having the spirit of Elijah.

President James E. Faust has said about this work: "Searching for our kindred dead isn't just a hobby. It is a fundamental responsibility for all members of the Church. We believe that life continues after death and that all will be resurrected. We believe that families may continue in the next life if they have kept the special covenants made in one of the sacred temples under the authority of God. We believe that our deceased ancestors can also be eternally united with their families when we make covenants in their behalf in the temples. Our deceased forebears may accept these covenants, if they choose to do so, in the spirit world" ("The Phenomenon That Is You," *Ensign*, Nov. 2003).

When you are unable to worship within the refuge of the

temple, I encourage you to spend some time searching for information about your ancestors on the Internet and ultimately submitting their names to the temple. Whether you are single and busy with your education or a career, married and have little children running about the house, or a bit older and feel pulled in dozens of directions, you can find those family members and help them get their sacred work performed in a house of the Lord. They may not speak to you directly like my son did to me—"Why haven't we done this before?"—but you may feel them with you, and their gratitude will be without words.

Our chapels are dedicated holy places of worship. In them, by the power of the priesthood, we partake of the sacrament, baptize eight-year-olds, bless babies, and set apart members to serve the Lord. We come together to grow in understanding of doctrine, share our testimonies of Jesus Christ and His Church, and be nourished by the Spirit.

Our buildings bless our communities as well as the people who attend. I remember visiting a small chapel up in the Peruvian highlands. The building was a sanctuary amidst the peaks of the Andes because of the worship of the faithful within.

We stand on holy ground in our homes. By the power of the priesthood, we can dedicate homes just as we dedicate temples and chapels. The environment of our homes—our conversation, music, television shows, books, and entertainment—establishes the ground on which we stand. May it be holy. May we have pictures on the walls of the Savior, temples, our families, our Church leaders, and favorite memories to serve as reminders that this is sacred ground.

In our homes, may we treat each other with kindness and respect, may we seek righteousness in what we do, and may our prayers be a measure of "Holiness to the Lord," as if that banner hung above our door.

Sister Rasband and I have traveled around the world. In Tacloban, Philippines, I wanted to get outside the chapel and into the homes of our members. The bishop took us to visit a beautiful Filipino family. We walked in the front door of their little tin home and saw two pictures on the walls, one of the Savior and one of the Manila Philippines Temple. There was a little mat on the dirt floor, where we knelt and prayed together. That is all they had, but let me say, it was enough. I have seen many homes from elegant mansions with the finest Picasso art to palaces of kings and queens. Yet, that home with that precious family embodied for me holy ground.

May we go forward in faith like this Filipino family; may we "be not troubled" as we stand in holy places and realize our promised blessings.

Consider this promise of President Nelson about the future: "I am optimistic about the future. It will be filled with opportunities for each of us to progress, contribute, and take the gospel to every corner of the earth. But I am also not naive about the days ahead. We live in a world that is complex and increasingly contentious. The constant availability of social media and a 24-hour news cycle bombard us with relentless messages. If we are to have any hope of sifting through the myriad of voices and the philosophies of men that attack truth, we must learn to receive revelation.

"Our Savior and Redeemer, Jesus Christ, will perform some of His mightiest works between now and when He comes again. We will see miraculous indications that God the Father and His Son, Jesus Christ, preside over this Church in majesty and glory" ("Revelation for the Church, Revelation for Our Lives," *Ensign*, May 2018).

I add my optimism to President Nelson's that as we stand on holy ground in our lives, we can find refuge from fear and move forward with faith.

2

KEEP YOUR PROMISES; TRUST THE LORD'S PROMISES

Ever mindful of our frailties in mortal life, the Lord has promised, "Be of good cheer, and do not fear, for I the Lord am with you, and will stand by you" (D&C 68:6). I have felt His presence when needing reassurance, comfort, or greater spiritual insight or strength. And I have been deeply humbled and been grateful for His divine companionship.

The Lord has said, "Every soul who forsaketh his sins and cometh unto me, and calleth on my name, and obeyeth my voice, and keepeth my commandments, shall see my face and know that I am" (D&C 93:1). That is perhaps His ultimate promise.

How important is it to you to keep your word? to be trusted? to do what you say you will do? to strive to honor your sacred covenants? to have integrity? How can that bring you peace? By living true to our promises to the Lord and to others, we walk the covenant path back to our Father in Heaven and we feel His love in our lives.

Our Savior, Jesus Christ, is our great Exemplar when it comes to making and keeping promises and covenants. He came to earth promising to do the will of the Father. He taught gospel principles in word and in deed. He atoned for our sins that we might live again. He has honored every one of His promises.

Can the same be said of each of us? What are the dangers if we cheat a little, slip a little, or do not quite follow through with our commitments? What if we walk away from our covenants? Will others come unto Christ in light of our example? Is your word your bond? Keeping promises is not a habit; it is a characteristic of being a disciple of Jesus Christ.

Consider, for example, Nephi's classic promise to "go and do." He wrote, "And it came to pass that I, Nephi, said unto my father: I will go and do the things which the Lord hath commanded, for I know that the Lord giveth no commandments unto the children of men, save he shall prepare a way for them that they may accomplish the thing which he commandeth them" (1 Nephi 3:7). Although it was uttered long ago, we in the Church stand on that promise today.

To "go and do" means rising above the ways of the world, receiving and acting on personal revelation, living righteously with hope and faith in the future, standing in holy places, making and keeping covenants to follow Jesus Christ, and thereby increasing our love for Him, the Savior of the world

A covenant is a two-way promise between us and the Lord. As members of the Church, we covenant at baptism to take upon us the name of Jesus Christ, to live as He lived. Our ministering one to another in the Church reflects our commitment to honor Him.

When we partake of the sacrament, we renew that covenant to take-upon us His name and make additional promises to improve. Our daily thoughts and actions, both large and small, reflect our commitment to Him. His sacred promise in return is, "If ye do always remember me ye shall have my Spirit to be with you" (3 Nephi 18:7).

My question today is, do we stand by our promises and covenants, or are they sometimes half-hearted commitments, casually made and hence easily broken? When we say to someone, "I will pray for you," do we? When we commit, "I will be there to help," are we? When we obligate ourselves to pay a debt, do we? When we raise our hands to sustain a fellow member in a new calling, which means to give support, assistance, and encouragement, do we?

One evening in my youth, my mother sat with me at the foot of her bed and spoke fervently of the importance of living the Word of Wisdom. "I know from the experiences of others, from years ago," she said, "the loss of spirituality and sensitivity

Our daily

thoughts and actions,

BOTH LARGE AND SMALL,

REFLECT

OUR COMMITMENT TO

HIM.

that comes from not following the Word of Wisdom." She looked right into my eyes, and I felt her words penetrate my heart: "Promise me, Ronnie [she called me Ronnie], today, that you will always live the Word of Wisdom." I solemnly made that promise to her, and I have held to it all these years.

That commitment served me well when I was in my youth and in later years when I was in business circles where substances flowed freely. I had made a decision in advance to follow God's laws, and I never had to revisit it. The Lord has said, "I, the Lord, am bound when ye do what I say; but when ye do not what I say, ye have no promise" (D&C 82:10). What is He saying to those who abide by the Word of Wisdom? That we will have the promise of health, strength, wisdom, knowledge, and angels to protect us (see D&C 89:18–21). We find safety, protection, peace, and other abundant blessings as we keep our promises.

Some years ago, Sister Rasband and I were at the Salt Lake Temple for the sealing of one of our daughters. As we stood outside the temple with a younger daughter not yet old enough to attend the ceremony, we spoke of the importance of being sealed in the holy temple of God. As my mother had taught me to do years before, we said to our daughter, "We want you safely sealed in the temple, and we want you to promise us that when you find your eternal companion, you will make a date with him to be sealed in the temple." She gave us her word.

She has since stated that our talk and her promise protected her and reminded her what was most important. She later made sacred covenants as she and her husband were sealed in the temple.

President Russell M. Nelson has taught: "We . . . increase the Savior's power in our lives when we make sacred covenants and keep those covenants with precision. Our covenants bind us to Him and give us godly power" ("Drawing the Power of Jesus Christ into Our Lives," *Ensign*, May 2017).

When we keep promises to one another, we are more likely to keep promises to the Lord. Remember the Lord's words: "Inasmuch as ye have done it unto one of the least of these my brethren, ye have done it unto me" (Matthew 25:40).

Reflect with me on examples of promises in the scriptures. Ammon and the sons of Mosiah in the Book of Mormon committed "to preach the word of God" (Alma 17:14). When Ammon was captured by Lamanite forces, he was taken before the Lamanite King Lamoni. He committed to the king, "I will be thy servant" (v. 25). When raiders came to steal the king's sheep, Ammon cut off their arms. So astonished was the king, he listened to Ammon's message of the gospel and was converted.

Ruth, in the Old Testament, promised her mother-in-law, "Whither thou goest, I will go" (Ruth 1:16). She lived true to her word. The good Samaritan, in a parable in the New

— WHEN WE —

keep promises to

one another,

WE ARE MORE LIKELY TO

keep promises

TO THE LORD.

Testament, promised the innkeeper that if he would care for the injured traveler, "Whatsoever thou spendest more, when I come again, I will repay thee" (Luke 10:35). Zoram, in the Book of Mormon, promised to go into the wilderness with Nephi and his brothers. Nephi recounted, "When Zoram had made an oath unto us, our fears did cease concerning him" (1 Nephi 4:37).

What of the ancient promise "made to the fathers" as described in the scriptures that "the hearts of the children shall turn to their fathers" (D&C 2:2; see also D&C 27:9; 128:17; Joseph Smith—History 1:39)? In the pre-earth life when we chose God's plan, we made a promise to help gather Israel on both sides of the veil. "We went into a partnership with the Lord," Elder John A. Widtsoe explained years ago. "The working out of the plan became then not merely the Father's work, and the Savior's work, but also our work" ("The Worth of Souls," *Utah Genealogical and Historical Magazine*, Oct. 1934, 189).

"[The] gathering is the most important thing taking place on earth today," President Nelson has said as he has traveled the world. "When we speak of the *gathering*, we are simply saying this fundamental truth: every one of our Heavenly Father's children, on both sides of the veil, deserves to hear the message of the restored gospel of Jesus Christ" ("Hope of Israel" [worldwide youth devotional, June 3, 2018], HopeofIsrael .ChurchofJesusChrist.org, 8).

In addition, as we keep our promises to the Lord, we can more easily trust the Lord and His promises. I know that all His promises will be fulfilled.

Your greatest strength is the Lord Jesus Christ. He has promised:

"I will be on your right hand and on your left" (D&C 84:88).

"I know my sheep, and they are numbered" (3 Nephi 18:31).

"[My] peace I leave with you, my peace I give unto you" (John 14:27).

"Come unto me ye blessed, for behold, your works have been the works of righteousness upon the face of the earth" (Alma 5:16).

"For they that are wise and have received the truth, and have taken the Holy Spirit for their guide, and have not been deceived—verily I say unto you, they shall not be hewn down and cast into the fire, but shall abide the day" (D&C 45:57).

This is why we should not be troubled by the turmoil of today, by those in the great and spacious building, by those who scoff at honest effort and dedicated service to the Lord Jesus Christ. Optimism, courage, even charity come from a heart not burdened by troubles or turmoil.

Spencer W. Kimball was one of the prophets of my youth. These past few years, after being called as an Apostle, I have found peace in his first message at general conference in October 1943. He was overwhelmed by his call; I know what that feels like. Elder Kimball said: "I did a great deal of thinking and praying, and fasting and praying. There were conflicting thoughts that surged through my mind—seeming voices saying: 'You can't do the work. You are not worthy. You have not the ability'—and always finally came the triumphant thought: 'You must do the work assigned—you must make yourself able, worthy and qualified.' And the battle raged on" (in Conference Report, Oct. 1943, 16–17).

I take heart from that pure-hearted testimony of this Apostle who would become the twelfth President of this mighty Church. He recognized he had to put behind him his fears in order to "do the work assigned" and that he had to rely on the Lord for the strength to make himself "able, worthy and qualified." We can too. The battles will rage on, but we will face them with the Spirit of the Lord. We will "be not troubled" because when we are true to our promises and stand with the Lord and stand for His principles and His eternal plan, we are standing on holy ground.

Now, what about that daughter and son-in-law who asked the very heartfelt and probing, fear-based question years ago about bringing children into this world? They seriously considered our conversation that night; they prayed and fasted and came to their own conclusions. Happily, and joyfully for them and for us, the grandparents, they have now been blessed with seven beautiful children as they go forward in faith and love.

As you go forward with faith, I invite you to consider the promises and covenants you make with the Lord, and with others, with great integrity, knowing that your word is your bond. I promise you, as you do this, the Lord will establish your words and sanction your deeds as you strive with unwearied diligence to build up your lives, your families, and The Church of Jesus Christ of Latter-day Saints. He will be with you, and you can, with confidence, trust the Lord and look forward to being "received into heaven, that thereby [you] may dwell with God in a state of never-ending happiness . . . for the Lord God hath spoken it" (Mosiah 2:41).

Take heart. Yes, we live in perilous times, but as we stay on the covenant path, keeping our promises and trusting in the Lord's promises, we need not fear. As we do so, we will not be troubled by the times in which we live or the troubles that come our way. Believe in the promises of Jesus Christ, that He lives and that He is watching over us, caring for us, and standing by us.

3

CREATE A FORTRESS
OF SPIRITUALITY AND
PROTECTION

When Jesus Christ appeared to the Nephites following His Crucifixion, He taught them the gospel and then encouraged, "Go ye unto your homes, and ponder upon the things which I have said, and ask of the Father, in my name, that ye may understand" (3 Nephi 17:3).

The counsel to "go ye unto your homes, and ponder" reminds us that Christ-centered homes are fortresses for the kingdom of God on earth in a day when, as prophesied, the devil "rage[s] in the hearts of the children of men, and stir[s] them up to anger against that which is good" (2 Nephi 28:20).

People have built fortresses throughout history to keep the enemy outside. Often those fortresses included a guard tower where watchmen—like prophets—warned of menacing forces and coming attacks.

In early Utah pioneer times, my great-grandfather Thomas

Rasband and his family were some of the first settlers to enter the Heber Valley in the beautiful Wasatch Mountains of Utah.

In 1859, Thomas helped construct the Heber fort, built for their protection. It was a simple structure of cottonwood logs positioned one next to the other, forming the perimeter of the fort. Log cabins were built inside the fortress using that common wall. The structure provided both security and safety for those pioneer families as they put down roots and worshipped the Lord. It was sacred ground.

So it is with us. Our homes are fortresses against the evils of the world. In our homes we come unto Christ by learning to follow His commandments, by studying the scriptures and praying together, and by helping one another stay on the covenant path. The new emphasis on personal and family study in the home through the curriculum *Come, Follow Me* is designed "to deepen our conversion and help us become more like Jesus Christ" (*Come, Follow Me—For Individuals and Families: New Testament 2019*, v). In so doing we will become what Paul called "new creature[s]" with our hearts and souls in tune with God (2 Corinthians 5:17). We need that strength to face and deflect the assaults of the adversary.

As we live with devotion born of faith in Jesus Christ, we will feel the peaceful presence of the Holy Ghost, who guides us to truth, inspires us to live worthy of the Lord's blessings, and bears witness that God lives and loves us. All this within the fortress of our own homes. But remember, our homes are only as powerful as the spiritual strength of each one of us within the walls.

President Russell M. Nelson has taught, "In coming days, it will not be possible to survive spiritually without the guiding, directing, comforting, and constant influence of the Holy Ghost" ("Revelation for the Church, Revelation for Our Lives," *Ensign*, May 2018). As the Lord's living prophet, seer, and revelator in this day, the watchman on the tower of our fortress, The Church of Jesus Christ of Latter-day Saints, he sees the advances of the enemy.

Make no mistake. We are at war with Satan for the souls of men. The battle lines were drawn in our pre-earth life. Satan and a third of our Father in Heaven's children turned away from His promises of exaltation. Since that time, the adversary's minions have been fighting the faithful who chose the Father's plan.

Satan knows his days are numbered and that time is growing shorter. As crafty and cunning as he is, he will not win. However, his battle for each one of our souls rages on.

For our safety, we must build a fortress of spirituality and protection for our very souls, a fortress that will not be penetrated by the evil one.

Satan is a subtle snake, sneaking into our minds and hearts when we have let our guard down, faced a disappointment, or

For our safety,

WE MUST BUILD A FORTRESS OF

SPIRITUALITY

—————— AND ——————

PROTECTION

for our very souls,

A FORTRESS THAT WILL NOT BE

PENETRATED BY THE EVIL ONE.

lost hope. He entices us with flattery, a promise of ease, comfort, or a temporary high when we are low. He justifies pride, unkindness, dishonesty, discontent, and immorality, and in time we can be "past feeling" (1 Nephi 17:45). The Spirit can leave us. "And thus the devil cheateth their souls, and leadeth them away carefully down to hell" (2 Nephi 28:21).

In contrast, we often feel the Spirit so powerfully as we sing praises to God with words like these:

> *A mighty fortress is our God,*
> *A tower of strength ne'er failing.*
> *A helper mighty is our God,*
> *O'er ills of life prevailing.*
>
> —"A Mighty Fortress Is Our God,"
> *Hymns*, no. 68

When we build a fortress of spiritual strength, we can shun the advances of the adversary, turn our backs on him, and feel the peace of the Spirit. We can follow the example of our Lord and Savior, who, when tempted in the wilderness, said, "Get thee behind me, Satan" (Luke 4:8). We each have to learn by the experiences of life how to do that.

Such righteous purpose is well described in the Book of Mormon when Captain Moroni prepared the Nephites to face attacks from a deceitful, bloodthirsty, power-hungry Amalickiah. Moroni constructed fortresses to protect the Nephites "that they might live unto the Lord their God, and that they might maintain that which was called by their enemies the cause of Christians" (Alma 48:10). Moroni "was firm in the faith of Christ" (v. 13) and was faithful "in keeping the commandments of God, . . . and resisting iniquity" (v. 16).

When the Lamanites came to battle, they were astonished by the Nephites' preparation, and they were defeated. The Nephites thanked "the Lord their God, because of his matchless power in delivering them from the hands of their enemies" (Alma 49:28). They had built fortresses for protection on the outside, and they had built faith in the Lord Jesus Christ on the inside—deep in their souls.

What are some ways we can fortify ourselves in troubled times, that we may be "instruments in the hands of God to bring about this great work"? (Alma 26:3). Let us look to the scriptures.

We are obedient. The Lord commanded Father Lehi to send his sons back to Jerusalem to "seek the records, and bring them down hither into the wilderness" (1 Nephi 3:4). Lehi did not question; he did not wonder why or how. Nor did Nephi, who responded, "I will go and do the things which the Lord hath commanded" (v. 7).

Do we act with the willing obedience of Nephi? Or are we more inclined to question God's commands as did Nephi's brothers, whose lack of faith eventually turned them away from the Lord? Obedience, exercised with "holiness of heart" (D&C 46:7), is what the Lord asks of us.

We trust the Lord, who said to Joshua as he prepared to lead the Israelites into the promised land, "Be strong and of a good courage; be not afraid, neither be thou dismayed: for the Lord thy God is with thee whithersoever thou goest" (Joshua 1:9). Joshua trusted those words and counseled the people, "Sanctify yourselves: for to morrow the Lord will do wonders among you" (Joshua 3:5). The Lord parted the waters of the Jordan, and the Israelites' forty years of wandering in the wilderness came to an end.

We trust the prophets, past and present. We do not know when the Savior will return, but this we do know: We must be prepared in heart and mind, worthy to receive Him, and honored to be part of all that was prophesied so long ago.

President Russell M. Nelson is the Lord's prophet on the earth, and at his side are his counselors in the First Presidency and members of the Quorum of the Twelve Apostles called of God. All are sustained as prophets, seers, and revelators. And the Restoration continues. I implore you, follow the inspired counsel of our dear prophet, President Nelson, his counselors and the Apostles, and other Church leaders. We are listening to the Lord and are on the front line of what is happening across the globe. When President Nelson announces new temples as he has done at each conference, he is signaling that the Lord is in charge of His work. The Church and its leaders are not deterred by troubled times.

Also, pay heed to the ancient prophets who foretold of our day, and you will be filled, deep in your hearts and souls, with the spirit and the work of the Restoration. I promise you will see the hand of God in your lives, hear His promptings, and feel His love.

This prophecy of Joseph Smith, the first prophet of the Restoration, is true and is being fulfilled: "No unhallowed hand can stop the work from progressing; persecutions may rage, mobs may combine, armies may assemble, calumny may defame, but the truth of God will go forth boldly, nobly, and independent, till it has penetrated every continent, visited every clime, swept every country, and sounded in every ear, till the purposes of God shall be accomplished, and the Great Jehovah shall say the work is done" (*Teachings of Presidents of the Church: Joseph Smith* [2007], 444).

We stand for the truth, as did the prophet Abinadi in the Book of Mormon. Arrested and brought before King Noah and his wicked priests, Abinadi taught of the Savior's Atonement and the Ten Commandments, and preached powerfully that Christ would "come down among the children of men, and . . . redeem his people" (Mosiah 15:1). He then, with faith deep within him, proclaimed, "O God, receive my soul" (Mosiah 17:19), and Abinadi "suffered death by fire" (v. 20).

We make and renew our covenants by partaking of the sacrament and by worshipping in the temple. Whether worshipping in a church building or at home under the direction of bishops and stake presidents or branch and district presidents, the sacrament is the centerpiece of our Sunday worship, where we are receiving the promise to "always have his Spirit to be with [us]" (D&C 20:77). With that sacred ordinance, we commit to take upon us the name of Jesus Christ, to follow Him, and to shoulder our responsibilities in this divine work as He did. In the temple or while doing family history work, we can "lay aside the things of this world" (D&C 25:10) and feel the Lord's presence and His transcendent peace. We can focus on our ancestors, our families, and eternal life in the presence of the Father. No wonder President Russell M. Nelson stated recently in Rome, "The good that will emanate from this temple is incalculably great" (in Tad Walch, "President Nelson Refers to Apostles Peter, Paul during Rome Temple Dedication," *Deseret News*, Mar. 10, 2019).

We should have integrity in all that we do. We should develop discernment and discipline so that we do not have to continually determine what is right and what is wrong. We should take to heart the words of Peter, the early Church Apostle, who cautioned, "Be sober, be vigilant; because your adversary the devil, as a roaring lion, walketh about, seeking whom he may devour" (1 Peter 5:8).

As we diligently strengthen our fortifications, we become like Jesus Christ, as His true disciples, with our very souls in His protection.

Your testimony of Jesus Christ is your personal fortress, the security for your soul. When my great-grandfather and his fellow pioneers built the Heber fort, they put up one log at a time until the fort was "fitly framed together" (Ephesians 2:21) and they were protected. So it is with testimony. One experience at a time, we gain a witness from the Holy Spirit as He speaks to our own spirit, teaching "truth in the inward parts" (Psalm 51:6). When we live the gospel of Jesus Christ, when we draw upon the Savior's Atonement and press forward with faith, not fear, we are fortified against the wiles of the adversary. Our testimonies connect us to the heavens, and we are blessed with "the truth of all things" (Moroni 10:5). And, like pioneers protected by a fortress, we are safely encircled in the arms of the Savior's love.

The prophet Ether taught, "Wherefore, whoso believeth in God might with surety hope for a better world, yea, even a place at the right hand of God, which hope cometh of faith, maketh an anchor to the souls of men, which would make them sure and steadfast, always abounding in good works, being led to glorify God" (Ether 12:4).

May you be blessed as you go forth with confidence in the Lord and in His gospel. Put your arms around those who stumble and, with the strength of the Spirit within you, lead them lovingly back to the fortress of spirituality and protection. Seek "to be like Jesus" in all that you do ("I'm Trying to Be like Jesus," *Children's Songbook,* 78); shun evil and temptations; repent, as we have been admonished by our dear prophet; be honest in heart; be upright and pure; show compassion and charity; and love the Lord your God with the devotion of a true disciple.

Our testimonies of the gospel of Jesus Christ, our homes, our families, and our membership in The Church of Jesus Christ of Latter-day Saints will be our personal fortresses of protection surrounding us and shielding us from the power of the evil one.

4

REMEMBER SPIRITUAL EXPERIENCES

While we must strive to do all in our power to build faith and spiritual fortifications, life is filled with surprises, disruptions, and challenges. At times we may feel our faith is faltering, not as strong or protective as it once was. What can we do to restore and rebuild testimony? Let me share a personal experience.

Not long ago, I met with a dear friend that I have known and loved for many years. When we met, my friend confided that he had been struggling. He felt he was experiencing, to use his words, a "crisis of faith" and sought my counsel. I felt grateful that he would share his feelings and concerns with me.

He expressed a great longing for what he had once felt spiritually and what he now thought he was losing. As he spoke, I listened carefully and prayed earnestly to know what the Lord would have me say.

My friend asked the question so poignantly phrased in the Primary song: "Heavenly Father, are you really there?" ("A Child's Prayer," *Children's Songbook*, 12). If you have been asking this same question, I would like to share with you the counsel I offered to my friend and hope that you may find your faith strengthened and your resolve renewed to be a committed disciple of Jesus Christ.

I begin by reminding you that you are a son or daughter of a loving Father in Heaven and that His love remains constant. I know that such reassuring feelings of love are difficult to recall when you are in the midst of personal battles.

Jesus Christ knows about fierce struggles and trials. He gave His life for us. His final hours were brutal, beyond anything we can even comprehend, but His sacrifice for each one of us was the ultimate expression of His pure love.

No mistake, sin, or choice will change God's love for us. That does not mean sinful conduct is condoned, nor does it remove our obligation to repent when sins are committed. But *do not forget*, Heavenly Father knows and loves each of you, and He is always ready to help.

As I pondered my friend's situation, my mind reflected on the great wisdom found in the Book of Mormon: "And now, my sons, remember, remember that it is upon the rock of our Redeemer, who is Christ, the Son of God, that ye must build your foundation; that when the devil shall send forth his mighty winds, yea, his shafts in the whirlwind, yea, when all his hail and his mighty storm shall beat upon you, it shall have no power over you to drag you down to the gulf of misery and endless wo, because of the rock upon which ye are built, which is a sure foundation, a foundation whereon if men build they cannot fall" (Helaman 5:12).

I testify that "the gulf of misery and endless wo" is a place no one wants to be. And my friend was feeling that he was on the edge.

In counseling individuals such as my friend, I have explored their decisions made over the years that led them to forget sacred experiences, to weaken their resolve to be righteous, and to doubt. I encouraged them, as I encourage you, to recall, especially in times of crisis, when you have felt the Spirit and your testimony was strong; remember the spiritual foundations you have built. I promise that if you will do this, avoiding things that do not build and strengthen your testimony or that mock your beliefs, those precious times when your testimony prospered will return again to your memory through humble prayer and fasting. I assure you that you will once again feel the safety and warmth of the gospel of Jesus Christ.

Each of us must first strengthen ourselves spiritually and then strengthen those around us. Ponder the scriptures regularly and remember the thoughts and feelings you experience as you read them. Seek other sources of truth as well, but heed this caution from the scriptures: "But to be learned is good *if* they hearken unto the counsels of God" (2 Nephi 9:29; emphasis added).

Ask your questions—you have them; we all do. Ask them of your parents, quorum leaders, Relief Society sisters, and others who have more experience, knowledge, and spiritual strength. Ask them in your mind and heart while you read the scriptures and wait to be taught by the Spirit. Ask the Lord in prayer and be patient for the answer.

Receive counsel from the leaders of the Church and follow them. They are wise, divinely guided servants of the Lord and able to see farther ahead; trust them. Attend Church meetings, especially sacrament meeting, and partake of the sacrament with a repentant and forgiving heart as you renew covenants, including the promise to always remember the Savior, that His Spirit may ever be with you.

Seek the power of the Atonement to strip away your follies so that you can sustain your strength. Encourage those close to you to do the same. We are less troubled when we are helping others rather than sliding into our own despair.

Ammon, in the book of Alma, reflected on his ministry wandering "in a strange land" (Alma 26:36). He wrote, "Now when our hearts were depressed, and we were about to turn back, behold, the Lord comforted us, and said: Go amongst

NO MATTER WHAT MISTAKES

WE HAVE MADE OR HOW IMPERFECT

WE FEEL WE ARE,

WE CAN ALWAYS BLESS
AND LIFT OTHERS.

REACHING OUT TO THEM IN

CHRISTLIKE SERVICE CAN HELP US

be not troubled.

thy brethren, . . . and bear with patience thine afflictions, and I will give unto you success" (v. 27).

Success comes in lifting others, teaching them truths, serving as an example of the power of the Atonement to heal and bless.

In addition, "bear with patience thine afflictions" acknowledges that times will be hard but that as we turn to the Lord, success—as He values success—will be ours. That success is making a difference in the lives of others, and in the process, we rescue both them and ourselves.

No matter what mistakes we have made or how imperfect we feel we are, we can always bless and lift others. Reaching out to them in Christlike service can help us be not troubled. We feel the love of God deep within our hearts bringing peace and comfort despite our own challenges.

It is important to remember the powerful counsel found in Deuteronomy: "Keep thy soul diligently, *lest thou forget* the things which thine eyes have seen, and lest they depart from thy heart all the days of thy life: but teach them thy sons, and thy sons' sons" (Deuteronomy 4:9; emphasis added).

Generations are affected by the choices we make. Share your testimony with your family; encourage them to remember how they felt when they recognized the Spirit in their lives and to record those feelings in journals and personal histories so that their own words may, when needed, bring to their remembrance how good the Lord has been to them.

You will recall that Nephi and his brothers returned to Jerusalem to obtain the brass plates that contained the recorded history of their people, in part so that they would not forget their past.

Also, in the Book of Mormon, Helaman named his sons after their "first fathers" so they would not forget the goodness of the Lord: "Behold, my sons, I desire that ye should remember to keep the commandments of God; . . . Behold, I have given unto you the names of our first parents who came out of the land of Jerusalem; and this I have done that when you remember your names ye may remember them; and when ye remember them ye may remember their works; and when ye remember their works ye may know how that it is said, and also written, that they were good. Therefore, my sons, I would that ye should do that which is good, that it may be said of you, and also written, even as it has been said and written of them" (Helaman 5:6–7).

Many today have the same tradition of naming their children after scriptural heroes or faithful ancestors as a way of encouraging them not to forget their heritage.

When I was born, I was given the name of Ronald A. Rasband. My last name honors my father's ancestral line. The middle initial *A* was given to me to remind me to honor my mother's Danish Anderson ancestry.

My great-great-grandfather Jens Anderson was from Denmark. And in 1861, the Lord led two Latter-day Saint missionaries to the Jens and Ane Cathrine Anderson home, where the missionaries introduced them and their sixteen-year-old son, Andrew, to the restored gospel. Thus began a legacy of faith of which my family and I are the beneficiaries. The Andersons read the Book of Mormon and were baptized a short time later. The following year, the Anderson family heeded the call of a prophet to cross the Atlantic to join the Saints in North America.

Sadly, Jens died on the ocean voyage, but his wife and son continued to the Salt Lake Valley, arriving on September 3, 1862. Despite their hardships and their heartaches, their faith never wavered, and neither has the faith of many of their descendants.

In my office hangs a painting[1] that captures so beautifully a symbolic reminder of that first meeting between my ancestors and those dedicated early missionaries. I am determined not to forget my heritage, and because of my name I will forever remember their legacy of faithfulness and sacrifice.

Never forget, question, or ignore personal, sacred spiritual experiences. The adversary's evil intent is to distract us from spiritual witnesses, while the Lord's desire is to encourage, enlighten, and engage us in His work.

---

1. The original painting was created by Christen Dalsgaard in 1856. The painting in my office is a copy created by Arnold Friberg in 1964.

Let me share a personal example of this truth. I distinctly recall a time when I received a prompting in answer to mighty prayer. The answer was clear and powerful. However, I failed to act immediately on the prompting, and after a period of time, I began to wonder if what I had felt had been real. Some of you may have fallen for that deception of the adversary as well.

Several days later, I awoke with these powerful verses of scripture in my mind: "Verily, verily, I say unto you, if you desire a further witness, cast your mind upon the night that you cried unto me in your heart. . . . Did I not speak peace to your mind concerning the matter? What greater witness can you have than from God?" (D&C 6:22–23).

It was as if the Lord was saying, "Now, Ronald, I already told you what you needed to do. Now do it!" How grateful I was for that loving correction and direction! I was immediately comforted by the prompting and was able to move forward, knowing in my heart that my prayer had been answered.

I share this experience to demonstrate how quickly our minds can forget and how spiritual experiences guide and sometimes redirect us. I have learned to cherish such moments "lest I forget."

To my friend, and to all who wish to bolster their faith, I give you this promise: as you faithfully live the gospel of Jesus Christ and abide by its teachings, your testimony will be protected, and it will grow. Keep the covenants you have made, regardless of the actions of those around you. Be diligent parents, brothers and sisters, grandparents, aunts, uncles, and friends who strengthen loved ones with personal testimony and who share spiritual experiences. Remain faithful and steadfast, even if storms of doubt invade your lives through the actions of others. Seek that which will edify and fortify you spiritually. Avoid counterfeit offerings of so-called "truths" that are so pervasive, and remember to record your feelings of "love, joy, peace, longsuffering, gentleness, goodness, faith, meekness, [and] temperance" (Galatians 5:22–23).

In the midst of life's greatest storms, *do not forget* your divine heritage as a son or daughter of God or your eternal destiny to one day return to live with Him, which will surpass anything the world has to offer. Remember the tender and sweet words of Alma: "Behold, I say unto you, my brethren, if ye have experienced a change of heart, and if ye have felt to sing the song of redeeming love, I would ask, can ye feel so now?" (Alma 5:26).

To all who feel the need to have their faith fortified, I plead with you, *do not forget!* Please do not forget.

Joseph Smith was a prophet of God. I know he saw and talked with God the Father and His Son, Jesus Christ, just as he recorded in his own words. How grateful I am that he *did not forget* to write of that experience, that we may all know of his testimony.

I know the Lord Jesus Christ lives and stands at the head of this Church. I pray that you and I will *never forget* sacred eternal truths—first and foremost, that we are sons and daughters of living and loving Heavenly Parents, who desire only our eternal happiness.

5

BECOME AN INSTRUMENT
IN THE LORD'S HANDS

The Lord draws us to Him not just to heal us but to help us become more like Him. The Book of Mormon is filled with examples of disciples who grew in spirituality and faith because they were instruments in His hands to further the plan of salvation.

President Thomas S. Monson, who called me to the holy apostleship in 2015, and who is remembered for encouraging us to reach out and rescue others, said: "We are surrounded by those in need of our attention, our encouragement, our support, our comfort, our kindness—be they family members, friends, acquaintances, or strangers. We are the Lord's hands here upon the earth, with the mandate to serve and to lift His children. He is dependent upon each of us. . . .

"'. . . Inasmuch as ye have done it unto one of the least of these . . . , ye have done it unto me' [Matthew 25:40]" ("What Have I Done for Someone Today?" *Ensign*, Nov. 2009).

Will we respond with love when an opportunity is before us to make a visit or a phone call, write a note, or spend a day meeting the needs of someone else? Or will we be like the young man who attested to following all of God's commandments: "All these things have I kept from my youth up: what lack I yet? Jesus said unto him, If thou wilt be perfect, go and sell that thou hast, and give to the poor, and thou shalt have treasure in heaven: and come and follow me" (Matthew 19:20–21).

The young man was being called to a greater service at the side of the Lord to do the work of the kingdom of God on earth, yet he turned away, "for he had great possessions" (Matthew 19:22).

What of our earthly possessions? For various reasons, they can be lost in just minutes. It is so important for each of us to strive to lay up our spiritual treasures in heaven—using our time, talents, and agency in service to God.

Jesus Christ continues to extend the call, "Come and follow me" (Matthew 19:21). He walked His homeland with His followers in a selfless manner. He continues to walk with us, stand by us, and lead us. To follow His perfect example is to recognize and honor the Savior, who has borne all of our burdens through His sacred and saving Atonement, the ultimate act of service. What He asks of each one of us is to be able and willing to take up the joyful "burden" of discipleship.

As members of the Church, we each have the sacred responsibility to "lift up the hands which hang down, and strengthen the feeble knees" (D&C 81:5).

How grateful the Lord is for each and every one of us, for the countless hours and acts of service, whether large or small, we so generously and graciously give each day.

King Benjamin taught in the Book of Mormon, "When ye are in the service of your fellow beings ye are only in the service of your God" (Mosiah 2:17).

President Russell M. Nelson has reached out demonstrably to world leaders, including those of the National Association for the Advancement of Colored People (NAACP). In a meeting in Salt Lake a few years ago, he and his presidency stood shoulder-to-shoulder with these great leaders. I introduced the press conference, where there was a marked "feeling of mutual respect and a desire to link arms." From that meeting have come opportunities to capitalize on the strengths of their organization and our Church and to help people by working together. Our prophet has reiterated that "the heartfelt conviction of our religion is that all people are God's children" (Russell M. Nelson, "NAACP Convention Remarks" [July 21, 2019], Newsroom.ChurchofJesusChrist.org). We have been building bridges together ever since.

President Nelson was slated to address the annual convention of the NAACP in Detroit, Michigan, in July 2019. The airport where he was to catch his plane was socked in with thick clouds, and the pilots could not land. They continued to circle as President Nelson suggested that the small group of us waiting should pray—right there on the tarmac. He explained the situation to our Father in Heaven and prayed for a miracle that the plane might land, that he might be able to speak to this very important group of people. He concluded, and what happened next was a miracle. The clouds parted just long enough for the plane to sweep down and pick us up. President Nelson was on the Lord's errand, and he had needed the Lord's help.

President Nelson is out in front on the Lord's instruction to love God with all our hearts and, then, to love our neighbors as ourselves (see Matthew 22:35–39).

Missionaries love those they teach. In 2005, at the conclusion of our son's mission in Kazakhstan, we met a solid, young convert he had introduced to the gospel. His name was Dmitriy Tsay. Fast forward to an assignment I had with Sister Rasband in Moscow in 2019. To our great shock and happy surprise, we encountered Dmitriy again. He is now not only a strong member of the Church, but he works for the Church as well on a wonderful assignment. The three of us connected with our son in the states by FaceTime and had a glorious reunion.

Dmitriy has been busy doing the Lord's work. Twenty members of his close family and friends in Kazakhstan and Russia have joined the Church. They watched him "glory in the Lord," and they responded to his invitations and his mission (Alma 26:16). Our son, Dmitriy, and tens of thousands of missionaries are setting their own lives aside to show love for God's children by sharing and living the gospel.

Focusing on serving our brothers and sisters not only comforts, lifts, and strengthens them; it can also guide us to make divine decisions in our own daily lives and prepares us to value and love what the Lord loves. He does not qualify the opportunity to make a difference in someone's life with the caveat—if we are having a particularly good day ourselves, "Come help." Instead He prompts us to break the cycle of discouragement and distress, recognizing that reaching out to others—"at all times and . . . in all places"—is a means to lifting our hearts as well (Mosiah 18:9).

That was the experience of Ammon when he was approaching the stiffnecked Lamanites: "Now . . . our hearts were depressed, and we were about to turn back," he explained (Alma 26:27).

How often do we turn away from the Lord's work because we are feeling low ourselves?

As we become more attuned to

responding to the Lord's errand,

WE WILL MORE OFTEN BE USED AS

 AN INSTRUMENT
IN HIS HANDS

TO DO HIS WORK.

Ammon continues: "Behold, the Lord comforted us, and said: Go amongst thy brethren, . . . and bear with patience thine afflictions, and I will give unto you success" (v. 27).

Success in Ammon's case came from being patient even in affliction and becoming an instrument in the Lord's hands. Jesus Christ knows our hearts and our heartaches, and He knows that strength, resilience, and comfort come from looking outside ourselves.

In so doing, we witness by our very lives that we are His disciples. When we are engaged in His work, we feel His Spirit with us. We grow in testimony, faith, trust, and love. We feel the peace and joy that come through helping others.

As we become more attuned to responding to the Lord's errand, we will more often be used as an instrument in His hands to do His work. Being an instrument in the Lord's hands is a unique calling for each one of us. We read of God using Gideon as "an instrument" to deliver the people of Limhi out of bondage (Alma 1:8). The sons of Mosiah traveled throughout Zarahemla "zealously striving to repair all the injuries which they had done to the church, . . . and explaining the prophecies and the scriptures to all who desired to hear them. And thus they were instruments in the hands of God in bringing many to the knowledge of the truth, yea, to the knowledge of their Redeemer" (Mosiah 27:35–36). Whereas Alma the Younger, strengthened by the Lord, slew Amlici, thereby becoming "an instrument in [the Lord's] hands to save and preserve [the] people" (Alma 2:30). The scriptures are replete with examples of the Lord using His chosen people as instruments in His hands to serve His purposes and further His work.

I dedicated the Durban South Africa Temple in 2020. That dedication and the Rome Italy Temple dedication were two of the most significant spiritual experiences of my life. I do not think I could be asked to do anything greater in my ministry than be assigned by the prophet of God to dedicate a temple.

Prior to the dedication, I had the opportunity to meet privately with the king and queen of the country of Lesotho, a landlocked nation within South Africa. Arranging the audience was a challenge, but fortunately it came through and we also were able to meet with members and missionaries in the area. Lesotho is a country of primarily Christian people. I presented the king and queen with an embossed leather edition of the Book of Mormon, and we had a wonderful visit. We talked about the oppression and persecution they had experienced since independence in 1966, and I told them about the early period of our Church when our people faced similar problems. After an hour, the king did not want to leave; we had become friends.

Now here is the miracle that can only be attributed to the Lord using the instruments He has to further His work.

At the same time that we were meeting with the royalty of this African nation, one of our missionary couples, Oscar and Carol McConkie, were working in Geneva, Switzerland, with the ambassadors and representatives of many nations. They approached the ambassador of Lesotho, a high-ranking official for that nation, and to their surprise, he wanted to talk not about government relations but about our doctrine—in particular, baptism.

By divine design, the Lord was orchestrating an introduction to the gospel of Jesus Christ for these two world leaders from the same country in two distant parts of the world. After receiving the missionary lessons, the ambassador, his wife, and their daughter were baptized members of the Church.

That is what happens when we make ourselves available to do the Lord's work. Lives are touched and changed one by one.

President Henry B. Eyring has taught: "The Lord knows both what He will need you to do, and what you will need to know. He is kind and He is all knowing, so you can with confidence expect that He has prepared opportunities for you to learn in preparation for the service you will give. You will not recognize those opportunities perfectly. . . . But when you put the spiritual things first in your life, you will be blessed to feel directed toward certain learning, and you will be motivated to work harder" ("Education for Real Life," *Ensign*, Oct. 2002). This has been so very true in my own life.

It was true in the life of Joseph Smith. He was studying in the book of James when he felt prompted to go into the woods to pray. We all know the passage. "I was one day reading the Epistle of James," he wrote, "first chapter and fifth verse, which reads: *If any of you lack wisdom, let him ask of God, that giveth to all men liberally, and upbraideth not; and it shall be given him*" (Joseph Smith—History 1:11).

Joseph Smith's school was in a grove of trees, near the family farm. As many have, I have walked the paths of that Sacred Grove. I have received a testimony of Joseph Smith's prophetic calling and felt the spirit of the Restoration of the gospel and the Church of Jesus Christ. Most recently, I have joined with the First Presidency and my fellow Apostles in the Quorum of the Twelve bearing witness through "The Restoration of the Fulness of the Gospel through Jesus Christ: A Bicentennial Proclamation to the World" in 2020. I testify to the truth of the marvelous vision the Prophet Joseph recounted: "I saw two Personages, whose brightness and glory defy all description, standing above me in the air. One of them spake unto me, calling me by name and said, pointing to the other—*This is My Beloved Son. Hear Him!*" (Joseph Smith—History 1:17).

I love those words. The Spirit testifies of truth, and Joseph's account is true. Notice Joseph's conclusion: "I had seen a vision; I knew it, and I knew that God knew it, and I could not deny it" (Joseph Smith—History 1:25).

What do *you* know? Do you have a testimony of the Prophet Joseph Smith, and that God the Father, Jesus Christ, and other heavenly messengers visited him? That he translated the Book of Mormon by the power of God? And that the gospel and priesthood keys were restored through him for these latter days? He was a young man, unschooled by the world's standards, but divinely prepared for his work on earth—"an instrument in the hands of God," who did "work mighty wonders, and [did] that thing which is great in the sight of God" (2 Nephi 3:24). Each one of us needs to know to our very core that Jesus is the Christ and that He has called prophets to lead us, beginning with Joseph Smith and continuing today with our dear President Russell M. Nelson.

Each of us needs to know of the truthfulness of the Book of Mormon and the power of priesthood keys that continue what began in upstate New York in a grove of trees. As an Apostle of the Lord Jesus Christ, I bear my witness that Joseph Smith saw God the Father and Jesus Christ, and They spoke with him. I bear my witness that the gospel was restored to the earth today and that the Book of Mormon is "the most correct of any book on earth" (introduction to the Book of Mormon). Make sure that you read, study, and ponder the words, and apply the teachings that are found in this sacred book of scripture.

I encourage you to regularly find quiet space and time to

search, ponder, and pray. When the rush, noise, and pressure of everyday life do not distract us, we can more easily connect with the Spirit of the Lord. The Lord has directed, "Pray always, and I will pour out my Spirit upon you, and great shall be your blessing" (D&C 19:38). That is why when we pray, we are distancing ourselves from the world by conversing with our Father in Heaven, in one-to-one communication.

The Lord teaches us individually, one at a time. The beauty of the gospel in our lives is that the Spirit touches our hearts one by one. We are baptized one by one into this Church. Never take that sacred experience lightly. Reflect on what it means for you—yourself—to be in one-on-one communication with the Lord as you get to partake of the sacrament each week.

We are given priesthood blessings one by one, whether for health, a new calling, comfort, encouragement, or at one of life's important passages. These are the words to us through one holding that sacred priesthood authority. We sustain one another in our callings, raising a hand to signify it, making a commitment to personally support one another. We are confirmed one by one, given a name and a blessing one by one. Reflect on those precious moments in your life when you and the Lord were one.

As you can tell, I love the expression "one by one." It is a divine teaching of the Lord Jesus Christ, who "went about doing

THE LORD TEACHES US INDIVIDUALLY,

ONE AT A TIME.

THE BEAUTY OF THE

GOSPEL IN OUR LIVES

— IS THAT —

the Spirit touches our hearts

ONE BY ONE.

good," touching the lives of people, one by one (Acts 10:38). Yes, there were large gatherings of those who followed Him to the mount where He taught, and there were large groups who trailed behind, hoping to hear His words and watch His miracles. Yet His parables, and often His healings, focused on the one.

One by one He took our sins upon Him in the Garden of Gethsemane. One by one He healed the blind, stooping for mud to apply to sightless eyes, or simply touching them with His finger. When the woman reached out in the throng for His cloak, He immediately said, "Who touched me?" (Luke 8:45). He felt her singular overture to Him, and she was healed amidst the press of all the people.

When four men carried their stricken friend to Jesus for healing, they had to lower his cot from the roof to get him in front of the Son of God. And then Jesus Christ healed him, one man borne by four friends. To the crippled man, who for so many years claimed his place at the pool of Bethesda amid the crush of others, Jesus said, "Take up thy bed, and walk. And immediately the man was made whole" (John 5:8–9).

One by one He lifts us to higher, safer ground. "May Christ lift thee up," Mormon wrote in a tender letter to his son, Moroni (Moroni 9:25).

Peter knew something about that. The Lord lifted him from the swirling sea as Peter cried out, "Lord, save me"

(Matthew 14:30). Jesus Christ reached out His hand for that one disciple. He has done so for every one of us here today. Time and time again we turn to Him and He is there, just for you and for me. Perhaps bringing peace, comfort, consolation, or inspiration. He has promised, "I will be on your right hand and on your left" (D&C 84:88). Ofttimes He provides that one-on-one moment of strength, wisdom, vision, or tenderness through another.

Just as He lifts, strengthens, and guides us, He asks us to do the same for others, without regard to race, gender, age, or circumstance. As Nephi taught, "All are like unto God" (2 Nephi 26:33).

The worth of a soul is best measured by the price paid for its redemption. The crowning work and glory of God is "to bring to pass the immortality and eternal life of man" (Moses 1:39). Would Christ have suffered in the Garden of Gethsemane, blood seeping from every pore, if each soul were not worth that price? Would He have submitted to brutality, humiliation, injustice, and scourging? Would He have allowed Himself to be hung on a cross among thieves and then buried in a borrowed grave if the worth of souls were not worth every-thing to Him?

And what of our Father in Heaven? Consider this teaching of President M. Russell Ballard: "There is no greater expression of love than the heroic Atonement performed by the Son of

God. . . . How grateful we should be that our Heavenly Father did not intercede but rather withheld His fatherly instinct to rescue His Beloved Son. Because of His eternal love for you and for me, He allowed Jesus to complete His foreordained mission to become our Redeemer. . . . Never, never underestimate how precious is the *one*" ("The Atonement and the Value of One Soul," *Ensign*, May 2004).

When the Lord Jesus Christ visited the people in the Americas, He extended this powerful invitation: "Have ye any that are sick among you? Bring them hither. Have ye any that are lame, or blind, or halt, or maimed, or leprous, or that are withered, or that are deaf, or that are afflicted in any manner? Bring them hither and I will heal them, for I have compassion upon you; my bowels are filled with mercy" (3 Nephi 17:7).

"And it came to pass that when he had thus spoken, all the multitude, with one accord, did go forth with their sick and their afflicted, and their lame, and with their blind, and with their dumb, and with all them that were afflicted in any manner; and he did heal them every one as they were brought forth unto him" (v. 9).

I love the account for it makes it clear, "He did heal them every one." This was not just about His miracles of healing; it was about His miracles of healing every one of them—one by one.

And then . . .

"He took their little children, one by one, and blessed them, and prayed unto the Father for them" (v. 21). Then he said, "Behold your little ones. . . . And they saw the heavens open, and they saw angels descending out of heaven as it were in the midst of fire; and they came down and encircled those little ones about, and they were encircled about with fire; and the angels did minister unto them" (vv. 23–24).

I believe in angels ministering to those in need. I have felt them. They are God's way of assuring us of spiritual presence and providing us with enhanced strength when we are desperately in need. He has promised "angels round about you, to bear you up" (D&C 84:88).

Some of those angels include each one of you. You are angels in the lives of so many. As you go about doing good, being an instrument in the Lord's hands, remember the Lord's words: "The worth of souls is great in the sight of God" (D&C 18:10). Remember, too, He was also talking about yours.

Everyone you meet, everyone in your family, everyone you work with—everyone in your professional and personal interaction has divinity within them, including you. We all may be suffering from mortal limitations, but we are all destined to be like God if we are worthy.

We will each be tested physically, emotionally, and spiritually. As we pray and fast, we will be strengthened and, like Nephi, we will be reminded "in whom [we] have trusted"

(2 Nephi 4:19). And in the process of those refiners' fires, we gain an increased measure of patience, humility, gratitude, resilience, and an ability to empathize with and help others.

In the words of Elder Orson F. Whitney, who served in the Quorum of the Twelve Apostles for twenty-five years: "To whom do we look, in days of grief and disaster, for help and consolation? . . . Men and women who have suffered, and out of their experience in suffering they bring forth the riches of their sympathy and condolences as a blessing to those now in need. Could they do this had they not suffered themselves?" (*Improvement Era*, Nov. 1918, 7).

Every one of us carries burdens and challenges, faces ailments and diseases, and needs special, individual care. That is how mortality refines us and grows our hearts to match the stature of our eternal souls.

I often think of our beloved pioneers who crossed the plains, burying children and loved ones along the way. It brings to mind a dearly beloved hymn that is so familiar and comforting to me: "Come, Come, Ye Saints." It is both poignant and promising.

> *And should we die before our journey's through,*
> *Happy day! All is well!*
> *We then are free from toil and sorrow, too;*
> *With the just we shall dwell!*

But if our lives are spared again
To see the Saints their rest obtain,
Oh, how we'll make this chorus swell—
All is well! All is well!

—*HYMNS*, NO. 30

I know "all is well." God lives, and Jesus Christ atoned for each one of us and provided an example for lifting others to higher and safer ground. I know that "the worth of souls is great in the sight of God" and that we can become like Him. May our lives reflect that sacred understanding as we respond to spiritual promptings and become an instrument in the Lord's hands.

6

CHOOSE AN ETERNAL PERSPECTIVE

In our challenges and trials, we experience a glimpse of Gethsemane. In the garden and in those days that followed, the Savior wrestled with our challenges, taking upon Himself all of that pain, and overcame all. His selfless sacrifice was for us that we might look to Him as our Exemplar, Savior, and Redeemer. When we draw upon the Atonement, we come to value Christ's strength in light of our weakness. We feel a measure of peace, hoping someday to be worthy to stand in the presence of the Father.

In the Grand Council in Heaven we chose to accept our Father's plan. It hinges on agency—the freedom to choose. Lehi taught his son Jacob, "For it must needs be, that there is an opposition in all things" (2 Nephi 2:11). We "are free to choose liberty and eternal life, . . . or to choose captivity and death" (v. 27). Our everlasting welfare is dependent on living the laws of God. His commandments are fixed; they do not change except as directed by revelation.

We chose to come to earth and receive a body. We committed to live the commandments that we might be worthy of eternal life, the greatest of all God's blessings. Central to our Father's plan was the mission of Jesus Christ and His Atonement that makes it possible for us to repent, be forgiven, and recommit to the covenant path. When all around us is in commotion, the Lord counsels, "Be still, and know that I am God" (Psalm 46:10). To be still is to trust that He has the power to vanquish not only our mistakes but the pain we feel as well. The very name of Jesus Christ speaks of salvation for all mankind. He is the "Son of the most high God" (1 Nephi 11:6), our "Redeemer, the Holy One of Israel" (1 Nephi 20:17), the "Saviour of the world" (John 4:42). Yet, His work and His ministry were never about Him. He sought only "to bring to pass the immorality and eternal life of man" (Moses 1:39). That is you and me.

Satan, on the other hand, presented his own plan that would have compelled us to live by his rules. His intent was to have us circle about him for his glory. Everyone who has lived or yet will live on this earth chose not to follow him. Satan has already lost more than we have right now. He does not have a body; he can never progress beyond where he is today; he can never be exalted. But still he continues to fight the war that he waged in heaven because he wants more than he has. He wants us to join him in his misery.

By divine design, we can become like Heavenly Father and receive all He has (see D&C 132:19–20). That promise means something on those days when things are not going right and we ask ourselves, "This is it?" Well, it is not. This is mortality, a stage of progression that guarantees for those who are righteous exaltation in the kingdom of God. Forever.

You probably feel like forever is too abstract, too far away. You may not feel you can even deal with today, and you may be dragging around your mistakes of yesterday as well. Perhaps students may say, "Let me tell you, Elder Rasband, about this monster of a class I have, and the lab requirements, and also my girlfriend just dumped me, and I can't figure out what I am good at so I don't have a major." Parents may lament that their children are rolling on the ground and pinching each other rather than quietly embracing *Come, Follow Me* on Sunday morning. Grandparents may find that quiet is harder to bear than children racing in and out of the back door with the dog. And those in care centers may face loneliness and boredom. Those overwhelmed with the state of their lives and the depression that consumes them may be thinking of suicide. And so it goes. Who is thinking about forever?

Well, brothers and sisters, you have the agency to look further than that. You have the capacity to become gods and goddesses in a realm that knows no sorrow and no defeat, that feels no pain and no rejection, that promises light and goodness and peace everlasting. You are "the children of light" (1 Thessalonians 5:5), and you must never let the darkness of today get in the way of your desire to be with God and become like Him.

With such uprightness comes joy. President Russell M. Nelson has said, "The joy we feel has little to do with the circumstances of our lives and everything to do with the focus of our lives.

"When the focus of our lives is on God's plan of salvation, . . . and Jesus Christ and His gospel, we can feel joy regardless of what is happening—or not happening—in our lives. Joy comes from and because of Him" ("Joy and Spiritual Survival," *Ensign*, Nov. 2016).

So, choose to feel joy because your Savior, Jesus Christ, has atoned for your sins and has felt your pain. For Him, the Atonement was a choice. He pled, "O my Father, if it be possible, let this cup pass from me: nevertheless not as I will, but as thou wilt" (Matthew 26:39). At that crucial moment, He submitted His will, His precious agency, to the Father, that the plan of happiness might go forward.

Choose to feel joy in your very existence as a child of God. That is not just a catchphrase in the Church or a song sung in Primary. Being a child of God means being connected to

YOU HAVE THE CAPACITY

—— TO BECOME ——

gods and goddesses

in a realm that knows no

sorrow and no defeat, that feels

no pain and no rejection,

—— THAT PROMISES ——

LIGHT AND GOODNESS

AND PEACE EVERLASTING.

the heavens while we journey in mortality. Being a child of God means there are expectations for us to make a difference in the Lord's kingdom—right now. Again, you have to look further than today's pleasures, disappointments, worldly accomplishments, or current trends to receive needed revelation from God. Do not be fooled; you are not of the world; you are divine.

My friends, you do not have to do this alone. The Holy Ghost, who is a member of the Godhead, will be your companion, guiding and directing you in quiet yet perfect ways. Take advantage of that counsel that reaches far beyond good ideas and worldly wisdom. Gain a testimony by the choices you make that the Holy Ghost "knoweth all things" (D&C 35:19) and shows "all things what ye should do" (2 Nephi 32:5).

Inherent in agency is obedience to God's commandments. As you strive for more serenity and joy—less fear and worry—will you follow one of the great themes of the Book of Mormon, that obedience brings great blessings?

In 2 Nephi, we read: "For the Lord God hath said that: Inasmuch as ye shall keep my commandments ye shall prosper in the land; and inasmuch as ye will not keep my commandments ye shall be cut off from my presence" (2 Nephi 4:4).

The Lord does not make that promise just once but time and again—in First, Second, Third, and Fourth Nephi, in Mosiah, Alma, Ether, Jarom, and Helaman. What the Lord makes clear is that we prosper when we live the commandments of God. When King Benjamin counseled his sons in the first chapter of Mosiah, he spoke of them having the Lord's "commandments always before [their] eyes" (Mosiah 1:5).

The Lord's commandments do not change. What He asked of Mary and Martha, Lehi and Nephi, He asks of us. King Benjamin describes it as having "no more disposition to do evil" (Mosiah 5:2). The thirteenth article of faith lays out a Christlike life with this declaration: "We believe in being honest, true, chaste, benevolent, virtuous, and in doing good to all men."

There was a time when most people believed and understood that they would be held accountable by God for living the commandments. Not so anymore. Few people observe the Sabbath with the reverence it deserves as the Lord's Day. Many consider charity, the pure love of Christ, to be simply a monetary donation. Others think nothing of taking God's name in vain; many squander the gifts He has given them in search of self-satisfying pleasures rather than following the Lord's pronouncement, "I came into the world to do the will of my Father" (3 Nephi 27:13).

But as disciples of Jesus Christ, we are different and determined. We seek to establish His righteousness and to reflect the blessings—including peace, happiness, and prosperity—that come from loving God and His ways.

AS DISCIPLES OF JESUS CHRIST,

WE ARE DIFFERENT AND DETERMINED.

WE SEEK TO

establish His righteousness and

to reflect the blessings—including peace,

happiness, and prosperity—

THAT COME FROM

LOVING GOD

AND HIS WAYS.

Never take casually your commitment to Jesus Christ and His commandments. Recognize that He is the "author and finisher of [your] faith" (Hebrews 12:2). Jesus Christ will be with you as you fulfill your commitments as a disciple, a believer, a faithful follower of Him, "the Son of the living God" (D&C 68:6).

So, when we are keeping the commandments, what does it mean to "prosper"?

Is it the measure of how much money we make? How many children we have? How many cars and trucks are sitting in our driveway? What positions we fill in our employment? Or even in the Church? To prosper in the Lord's way is neither an academic discussion nor a measure of worldly goods.

I believe the Lord needs each one of us to prosper on the front lines of our professions, in our community involvement—which includes actively working to keep our freedom of religion and religious liberties and keeping up with our responsibilities as honest, compassionate, fair-minded citizens—and as leaders in our families and in our faith. The Lord needs us to "[wax] strong in the knowledge of the truth" (Alma 17:2) and to be examples of how living the gospel of Jesus Christ brings contentment, fulfillment, and calm.

But if we measure by the world, if financial gain lures us over to the great and spacious building, if it prompts us to edge into the mists of darkness, if it compromises our ability to lead our families along the iron rod, it will never be worth the price.

Consider these three ways we may prosper:

First, to have faithful family, friends, and mentors in relationships that lift us, guide us, and prompt us to do the same for others.

Second, to turn to our Father in Heaven in prayer, making Him an important part of our decisions and direction. In that way, we are divinely connected to His guidance and goodness.

Third, to live the commandments so that we have the blessing of the Lord's Spirit in our lives.

To illustrate the first point, I would like to share a little about my beginnings and the influence of faithful family and friends. I prospered as a youth, growing up in a very humble home where the Spirit was in abundance. I met my dear sweetheart, Melanie Twitchell, when we were in college. We dated and then were married in the Salt Lake Temple, sealed for time and all eternity. We have been blessed in our love for one another and our love for our Father in Heaven and His plan of salvation. We chose to start our family shortly after we were married, having confidence that we would be blessed in our temporal matters if we put the Lord first. We determined our lives would be committed to serving the Lord and learning His ways, including serving and caring for others. I have come to appreciate the Lord's promise, "I will lead you along" (D&C 78:18).

Just as we appreciate being lifted and strengthened by others, we also strive to reach out to "mourn with those that mourn, . . . and comfort those that stand in need of comfort" (Mosiah 18:9). There was a time when I was on assignment in Santa Rosa, California, where whole communities had been devastated by fire. Everything had gone up in flames. Their homes, clothes, cars, computers, scrapbooks. Everything. As we visited with these dear brothers and sisters, I learned about sifting—they actually had large sifters for people to use, sifting through the ashes, hoping to find a wedding ring, a photo, any precious treasure or memory that might have survived the devastating fires.

I stood with a small group looking at the scorched land where whole neighborhoods once stood. I could have been in meetings, but it was far more critical to be standing right there with them and letting them know we loved them and that we were praying for them.

They had nothing. But they had each other, and you can imagine how touched and grateful I was to see their strength and hear their prayers in such difficult times.

The situation was similar in Beaumont–Port Arthur, Vidor, and Port Neches, Texas, where Hurricane Harvey had flooded homes. Again, so little could be salvaged. As I went to the neighborhoods and met with the people, my heart was saddened for those who had lost so much but grateful to watch the united efforts of missionaries and members—some who had come great distances to help in the cleanup efforts. There was so much to do. I learned a new term in Texas as well—mucking! That is what they called it as they were removing everything from their homes—everything, including walls, floors, ceilings, and furniture—and at the same time wading through deep mud and water searching for treasures and memories. Our hearts were heavy for these dear brothers and sisters.

Did their disobedience bring the winds, rain, fire, and floods? No. Certainly, there are times when the Lord chastens His people and some pose the question, "Why do bad things happen to good people?" I do not know. Perhaps the answer is because tragedies bring forth opportunities to serve and lift and teach eternal principles, because there is opposition in all things, and because this is mortal life, subject to the traumas of earthly existence.

The Lord has made it clear that we prosper when our associations and relationships are framed in living the commandments of God.

The second point is that prayer plays an important part in helping us prosper.

In Alma, we read: "And they did pray unto the Lord their God continually, insomuch that the Lord did bless them, according to his word, so that they did wax strong and prosper in the land" (Alma 62:51).

Praying for others, even those we do not know, will bring down power from on high. The heavens open not with replacements of what has been lost or compromised, but with God's love and peace. The power of the Atonement, the rock upon which we build, brings us peace in troubled times. I saw it happen in California and in Texas. We will see it in our lives when we face daunting challenges.

A few years ago, I was in Harlem, New York, an area I supervised as a mission president. I was participating in the twentieth anniversary celebration of the Church in Harlem. A piece of my heart and a piece of my testimony are still there. We had prayed long and hard for miracles in Harlem.

In 1997, Church leaders formed the Manhattan Ninth Branch, better known as the Harlem Branch. Several days before the dedication of the Manhattan New York Temple in 2004, construction began on a Church-built meetinghouse in Harlem. Three wards meet in that building today. One of our missionaries, who served in that area, is now a bishop there.

We had prayed earnestly for guidance; we had pleaded with our Heavenly Father for His divine help to build the Church in Harlem— and what happened? Our prayers were answered, and the Church prospered over time, though not all at once.

The third point is that obedience to the Lord's commandments makes us worthy and able to be in His presence. That happens most directly in the temple. Remember in the scriptures the Lord's caution that the consequence of disobedience is being "cut off from [His] presence" (2 Nephi 4:4).

In the temple, we renew our spiritual perspective. In the temple, we recommit our lives to the Lord. In the temple, we recognize "things as they really are, and . . . things as they really will be" (Jacob 4:13).

President Thomas S. Monson has said: "Come to the temple and place your burdens before the Lord and you'll be filled with a new spirit and confidence in the future. Trust in the Lord, and if you do He'll hold you and cradle you and lead you step by step along that pathway that leads to the celestial kingdom of God" ("San Diego Temple: 45th house of the Lord dedicated in 'season for temple building,'" *Church News*, May 8, 1993).

Temples bring to families and individuals an opportunity to draw closer to the Lord Jesus Christ and our Father in Heaven. In the temple, we can obtain a more eternal perspective. Always have a current temple recommend and count it a great honor to be worthy. Go to the temple often and you will prosper with the Spirit of the Lord in your lives.

The Saints in Italy waited a long time for a temple.

I treasure the time spent at the Rome Italy Temple dedication. It, like all temples, stands as "the great symbol of our membership" (Howard W. Hunter, *Ensign*, Oct. 1994). First, I joined Elder Bednar as we took dignitaries on tours

ALWAYS HAVE A CURRENT

TEMPLE RECOMMEND

AND COUNT IT A GREAT HONOR

TO BE WORTHY.

GO TO THE TEMPLE OFTEN

— AND —

YOU WILL PROSPER

with the Spirit of the Lord

in your lives.

at the open house. Sister Rasband and I hosted a delegation from the Roman Catholic Church and the Vatican. I was concerned how the Catholic Church would welcome our temple in Rome. But we immediately felt their love and received their best wishes. We explained that temples did not originate with the Latter-day Saints. Solomon's temple and Herod's temple were built in early times. We described that from the Book of Mormon we know that the people of the Americas built temples and that the Savior appeared after His Resurrection at one of the temple sites. We talked of the majestic design, the finest materials, and the very best workmanship. When one of the delegation of Catholic leaders asked what basis in scripture we had for baptisms for the dead, I recalled a passage learned as a young missionary and said, "Else what shall they do which are baptized for the dead, if the dead rise not at all? why are they then baptized for the dead?" (1 Corinthians 15:29).

The brother responded, "Elder Rasband, I have never considered that scripture this way before." Privately in my heart I rejoiced.

At the conclusion of our tours, Sister Rasband and I took turns bearing testimony that the temple is the great symbol of our membership and that everything in the Church culminates in eternal marriage and the creation of eternal families. I was speaking for all of us, all in the Church whose witness of temple blessings is real in their lives. The temple gives us eternal perspective.

While there, Sister Rasband reflected on what made Rome so extremely special. She mused, "What was I feeling? Was it the joy of the Italians to finally have a house of the Lord in their country? Was it the symbol of the oval representing eternity, depicted in the shape of the temple and found throughout its celestially beautiful halls, a constant reminder of the eternal covenants made in the house of the Lord? Was it the wonderful temple piazza with magnificent 500-year-old olive trees that took our hearts back to Gethsemane, where the Lord bled for each of us? Perhaps it was walking beside the cascading fountain that ran through the center of the piazza to the visitors' center, reminding us of Christ's offered living water, as it led us to the welcoming arms of the magnificent Thorvaldsen-replica statue of the Christ, and behind Him the original Twelve Apostles who took the gospel out to the world to fulfill the work that their Savior had commanded them to do, or the magnificent curved art glass with the Savior standing in the center, His foot pointed towards us and His hand reaching out to us, welcoming all to come unto him (see 3 Nephi 9:14)?" Her question was answered: All of these things contributed to the powerful spirit of being at the Rome Italy Temple, because they all bore witness that Jesus is the Christ!

At one point, Elder David A. Bednar and I visited the

Mamertine Prison in Rome, where the Apostles Peter and Paul supposedly were imprisoned. In that prison, in a dungeon two levels underground, we observed the little rock stump where Paul was chained for two years. You can imagine how that made us feel. The assurances of the gospel and God's eternal plan sustained him in that terrible time. Was he troubled about his situation? I am sure he was. But was he troubled about his own standing with the Lord? Absolutely not, because he had been a faithful instrument in the work of God.

At the Rome Italy Temple Visitors' Center, all the prophets and apostles on the earth today, all fifteen of us, had our picture taken in our white suits surrounding the *Christus* with the statues of the early Apostles behind us. President Nelson went and stood next to Peter, the senior Apostle in the row, who had carved in his statue at his side a ring of keys representing the keys of the priesthood. We all marveled that those same keys were returned to the earth by Peter when he conferred them on Joseph Smith, and that now President Nelson, the seventeenth president of the restored Church, holds those keys.

It was a remarkable setting, a "hinge point in history," with such a presence and power of the priesthood of God. As if in unison, prophets—present and past—were reaffirming that the Lord's Church, The Church of Jesus Christ of Latter-day Saints, is on the earth, and "these are our days."

I have identified three things that will help you prosper in the years ahead, despite challenging and perilous times: One—pay attention to those with whom you associate—your family, friends, fellow workers, neighbors, and Church members. Two—pray for guidance in your decisions and follow promptings. And three—be obedient to God's commandments so that you may be worthy to attend the temple—His holy house.

This pattern for your life will bring blessings as described in Mosiah: "And they were called the people of God. And the Lord did pour out his Spirit upon them, and they were blessed, and prospered in the land" (Mosiah 25:24).

May you know and feel the importance of your life in the Lord's kingdom here on earth. May you have the wisdom to make good choices and to keep the commandments, to think beyond the vagaries of today to the profound and eternal opportunities that await you, as you choose to follow the Son of God. As you do, may you receive the blessings of peace, joy, and prosperity, even amid the challenges of this mortal life. May you have charity for all, whether inside or outside your circle, and the strength to live with devotion the doctrines of Almighty God.

CONCLUSION

"BE NOT TROUBLED"

God knew that in mortality we would have challenges set before us—seeming mountains piled on mountains, mountains of our own making, mountains in every direction. He also knew we would need respite from the climb. We find that peace in Jesus Christ, His Atonement, His Church, and His teachings. He promised peace "not as the world giveth, give I unto you" (John 14:27).

When Jesus Christ says, "Be still, and know that I am God" (Psalm 46:10), His words reflect the promise, "Be not troubled." He who calms the seas will calm our hearts, shelter us in His arms, comfort us on our very bad days, and heal our wounds. Mormon's words to his son Moroni are important for us all: "May Christ lift thee up, and may his sufferings and death, and the showing his body unto our fathers, . . . and the hope of his glory and of eternal life, rest in your mind forever . . . , and abide with you forever" (Moroni 9:25–26).

With the Atonement of Jesus Christ, His Church, His gospel, and our connection to Him in the heavens, we may always have hope for better days.

In the Garden of Gethsemane, the Savior wrestled on our behalf. That is why He is able to empathize and feel the depth of our challenges, afflictions, and sins. King Benjamin, in his mighty speech outside the temple, related words of the Savior's Atonement given Him by an angel: "And lo, he shall suffer temptations, and pain of body, hunger, thirst, and fatigue, even more than man can suffer, except it be unto death; for behold, blood cometh from every pore, so great shall be his anguish for the wickedness and the abominations of his people" (Mosiah 3:7).

His selfless sacrifice was for us that we might look to Him as our Exemplar, Savior, and Redeemer. He knew we could do it. As we receive the blessings of His Atonement, we come to value Christ's strength in light of our weaknesses. Our Savior beckons time and again, "Come unto me, all ye that labour and are heavy laden, and I will give you rest" (Matthew 11:28). That rest is life eternal.

I have been with you in your chapels, your homes, and your communities around the world. I have witnessed your goodness and been blessed by your testimonies and your desire to serve. Remember, troubles diminish as we do the Lord's bidding. Be courageous, resilient, and compassionate as you do His sacred work.

I promise as an Apostle of God that you will be not troubled as you are renewed by His love, patience, assurance, and mercy. Remind yourself when things are hard, "these are my days," and make the most of them in helping prepare for the Second Coming of our Lord and Savior Jesus Christ.

You are in the Lord's hands. You are instruments in this great work and sons and daughters of a loving Father in Heaven. I pray you will be not troubled as you go forward with faith and commitment, with love for the Lord and His work, and with the devotion of a true disciple.